BROKEN: TEEN SCARS

T.D. Series Book 2

Patricemfoster.com

by

Patrice M Foster

This book is a work of fiction. This book is not intended or meant to replace sound medical advice. Any resemblance to actual events or locales or persons, living or dead, is entirely coincidental.

Broken Teen Scars

ISBN: 9780998187419
Library of Congress Control Number: 2016917819
Cover design By **Keri Knutson @alchemybookcovers.com**

Table of Contents

Introduction

You are about to read the story of the life of a young woman named Esther. It is a story she is going to tell you in her own words, but before you read it, you should understand a few very important facts about her struggles and the scars they left. They are not scars you can see, and they may sound like scars you have too, or maybe they sound like scars that a friend carries.

The first fact is that Esther is someone who suffers from *depression*. This is different from being sad or unhappy. As one expert said: "Feeling unhappy or sad in response to disappointment, loss, frustration, or a medical condition is normal. Many people use the word 'depression' to explain these kinds of feelings, but that is really situational depression, which is a normal reaction to events around us." (https://www.ineedalighthouse.org/depression-suicide/teen-depression/)

So, Esther is not someone who is just sad a lot or who is disappointed from time to time. What

Esther suffers from is *clinical depression,* and it is a condition that can be overwhelming and never-ending. It left her feeling completely broken inside.

You will hear Esther describe herself as feeling like she was "living in the center of a black hole in the middle of a faraway universe" and like she was "doomed" to life on the streets.

LIFE WITH DEPRESSION

She was unable to shake off the despair, loneliness, and sense of being isolated, but this is not the only way that someone with depression feels. Others with depression say they feel lifeless or empty; they say they cannot experience anything, even pleasure. Many people with depression say that they are "going through the motions" and that it is as if they are not actually alive.

When someone says "going through the motions," it means just as it sounds. You are doing something without really feeling anything.

As an example, imagine wrapping up gifts for people. It is really fun and exciting, and it can be difficult to do a great job at it if the gifts have odd shapes or are really big, but as you wrap them, you imagine the moment when the gifts are opened and consider how happy the person who got the gifts will be.

However, if you are depressed and just going through the motions, you won't have many thoughts as you wrap the gifts, and even if you do a good job, you will hardly pay attention. You will just do it like a machine and feel no excitement, joy, or anticipation. You make motions, but you don't get anything out of those motions.

That is what Esther struggles with every day.

Esther's depression actually led her to life on the street, and to total isolation from her mother and father, brother and sisters - and worst of all, from herself. She did not return to herself until she had gone through her own personal nightmare, but the most important thing to know is that Esther chose to change and get better.

SOME FACTS ABOUT DEPRESSION

Why do people like Esther - who is from a middle-class family of well-educated people - become depressed?

It happens for a lot of different reasons, and it happens to everyone. It is very common in teenagers, but the teens are all different ages, races, and from all economic backgrounds. That means that a poor white boy is just as likely to be depressed as a rich black boy or girl.

Experts say that there is not just one reason for it, and it can be caused by genetics, medical conditions, and brain chemistry. It can also be caused by life events, a person's outlook, and even changes in the seasons!

One thing all experts know is that it is a serious "health condition that needs treatment, just like asthma or diabetes." (http://kidshealth.org/en/teens/why-depressed.html)

DEPRESSION IS A HEALTH CONDITION

Take a second to think about that. Do you think of someone who has a mental health problem as a person who needs special medicine and treatment by a doctor? Many people don't look at mental health the same way they do something like asthma. Instead, they think of it as "something wrong" with the person struggling with something like depression.

That is what is known as a "stigma," and it is a big problem for everyone, but most especially for those with any sort of mental health condition. A stigma means that "shame or disgrace is attached to something regarded as socially unacceptable"; they are often very unfair.

Should someone with asthma feel shame? Should they feel that their condition is socially unacceptable? No, and it is how we should all see mental health conditions like depression.

Someone with depression can't just "cheer up" when someone tells them to. They can't "cut it out" or "stop being difficult." They are dealing with a medical issue that they cannot control any more than someone with asthma can help having their serious breathing trouble.

It may help to understand Esther's story if you understand depression better.

We know it is a mental health condition, and doctors know that it actually changes the chemistry in the brain. Chemicals in our brains, called neurotransmitters, send different messages to nerves inside our brains, and some of these chemicals control how we feel. Depression makes the brain produce a lot less neurotransmitters, and this creates an imbalance in the brain.

When a doctor treats you for depression, he or she is going to give you special medicine that puts the brain's chemistry back into a healthy balance. You won't be able to do this on your own, and you need help to find out why your brain is not producing the right amount of neurotransmitters and then get the right medicines to restore balance.

What if someone with depression does not get treatment? For a teenager like Esther, it is a very serious problem. Depression puts young people at great risk for suicide, but most especially when they are abusing alcohol and drugs, when they are socially isolated, and when depression continues without any sort of treatment.

And if you are a teen or young adult struggling with depression right now, you should know that you are not alone. Just consider some of the statistics about teen depression:

- Approximately 20 percent of teens will experience depression before they reach adulthood.
- Between 10 and 15 percent of teenagers have some symptoms of depression at any one time.
- Depression increases a teen's risk for attempting suicide by 12 times.
- 30 percent of teens with depression also develop a substance abuse problem.
- Depressed teens usually have a smaller social circle and take advantage of fewer career and educational opportunities.
- Depressed teens are more likely to have trouble at school and in jobs, and to struggle with relationships.

(https://www.ineedalighthouse.org/depression-suicide/teen-depression/)

So, understand that all of the negative things you might believe or think about yourself are untrue. It is not YOU…it is the depression that is making it hard for you to go out with friends or to do your studies. It is the depression that is making you want to use drugs or consume alcohol.

Of course, that also means it is ONLY YOU who can choose to fight the depression and improve your life. You do this with the help of doctors and therapists, as well as friends, family, and others. Among the most important relationships you can create to help overcome depression is the one with other people fighting the same battle. Esther decided to share her story to help other teens and young adults after someone else with depression helped her to recover. Sharing your stories, or hearing stories from other people with depression, really helps.

You will hear Esther tell you about her suicidal thoughts, her isolation, and her struggles in all of her relationships - even with her parents. The good news is that you are also going to hear about Esther's recovery and success. You will see that she experienced many scary and difficult things, but that she decided to overcome every obstacle and change for the better. She had help from counselors and doctors, but also from other people suffering with depression.

She also had help from people who work with homeless youth. You see, Esther was up against two huge issues - depression *and* homelessness.

WHEN YOU ARE HOMELESS

The statistics about homelessness are even scarier than the statistics about depression. After all, homeless youths face very bad short- and long-term consequences, which include mental health problems like depression, alcohol and drug abuse, suicidal thoughts, and more. They are also more "likely to engage in 'survival sex' - trading sex to gain food, clothing, drugs, money, or just for a safe place to sleep at night."

(http://www.safehorizon.org/page/homeless-youth-statistics--facts-69.html)

You will see that this is exactly what happened to Esther.

Because her home life and family life were miserable, cold, and full of rejection, she suffered untreated and undiagnosed depression. This forced her to run away to escape the emotional pain, and she ended up on the street, selling herself and abusing alcohol to survive.

I don't want to tell the whole story - that is Esther's job - but I did want you to begin reading her words once you knew some facts. The statistics don't lie, and it is amazing that Esther survived to share her story and help others.

You will see that she is an incredibly strong, smart, and brave person. She has come a long way since she ran away from home several years ago. You will see that depression is nothing to be ashamed of, and that it can be treated when you get the help you need. Of course, you will also see that it has to start with YOU.

To learn these important lessons, let's meet Esther and hear all about her journey from that black hole in some far-off universe back to a healthy and happy life here on Earth.

Chapter One

MEET ME

"You sound so exotic," said the pretty blonde girl.

That was cool; I liked hearing that about myself, especially because of the things I had to hear about myself at home.

What I heard at home was: "Esther, why do you have to be so difficult? Why can't you just study like your sisters and brother?"

And hearing this almost every day is one of the reasons I left home at the age of 17.

"If you are going to be a lawyer, you cannot get into a good college with nothing but C's and D's on your report card," my father shouted anytime he saw me doing anything other than studying.

"I never said I wanted to be a lawyer," I argued.

His answer was always the same: "Who says what you say or think matters? You are under our roof, and you will do what we tell you. We know best."

The thing is, they *didn't* really know best.

In the years that have passed since I left home, I understand things a lot more clearly. When I was 17, though, and struggling to figure out who I was, I was living in a pretty miserable place inside myself. I wanted to be an artist, not a lawyer. All of my schoolwork was uninteresting to me, and I hardly tried to pass any of my classes.

I didn't know then that my behavior was a way of coping with the pressure, stress, and rejection I was living with at home. So, I did badly in school, and it made my parents, especially my father, angrier and angrier. Soon, it was like he was disgusted just from looking at me.

To look at my family, though, you might believe that I really was being difficult. After all, I come from an educated family. My parents are a success story, and it did seem that I was a major black sheep for being born "the creative one."

Perhaps that is why the white girl telling me that I was exotic made me so happy. And why did that girl say I seemed "exotic"? Why not cool or different, or even funky?

Well, my dad is from Haiti, and my mother is from Germany. We had come to the United States, with my three sisters and little brother. We all have accents, but my English is great. That was one of the subjects I always studied and passed because I always wanted to be in America and become a famous artist here.

I have big, curly black hair and honey colored skin. I have always loved art. I tend to get interested in anyone who seems artistic or just unusual. I try to dress in a way that says "creative artist" too.

If you want to talk about painting, drawing, sculpture, or just the way the colors in the sky look…well, that is something I want to talk about too! Not history, politics, geometry, or other school subjects.

So, maybe she was right. I am exotic, right? I'm a black immigrant teen in the United States, with a unique family and an artistic temperament. Yet none of that was obvious to me when I was a teenager. Instead, I felt constantly stressed out and really deeply depressed, and it all had to do with the fact that I had a deep sense that I didn't belong. In fact, I felt like I couldn't belong.

RUNNING AWAY FROM MYSELF

Do you know what happens to some people who believe they cannot belong where they are? Sometimes, people who are convinced that they don't fit in, start acting like they don't fit in.

My sisters and brothers were "perfect"; they got good grades, did what my parents told them to do, and never asked "why?". I was the opposite, and it made me miserable.

So, what did I do about it? Rather than just sticking to my dream of becoming an artist and proving to my parents that this was realistic and a positive thing, I simply defied them.

I didn't try at school. In fact, I refused to do my work and just barely scraped by. I hated my school uniform, so I did alterations to it, shortening the skirt, cutting the neckline of the sweaters and tops, changing the sleeves…and always getting in trouble for it.

I started to do really bad things, because that's what they expected from me, right? I was no good, a failure, and a disgrace, so why not actually become all of those things?

I started to lie. I would wear my school uniform and head out the door like I was going to school, but that was a lie. Instead, I would stop somewhere and change my clothes. Then, I would meet up with older kids who also skipped school, and we'd all go to places to steal things and then sell them online or to a street guy for cash.

We all started to drink a lot of alcohol, and some of the kids got into drugs. I started hanging out with older boys, and then guys who were legally men and way too old for me. I started to have sex with a lot of guys, and I always wanted them to like me for it, but none of them ever did.

I flunked out of school, and soon after that, I left home. I didn't do it in a way that was smart or safe. I just ran away.

And you know what? The whole time, I was just running away from myself. I couldn't be what my parents wanted, and so I ran away from them. I couldn't get boys to like me, and so I stopped hanging around with them. I couldn't get men to like me, and so I started to do really bad things.

I soon began to break the law in ways that I now cannot believe I did. It was like I was another person! Then things got much, much worse. It was only when I was in the darkest and most desperate place that a small voice began to whisper inside of me. And finally, I was ready to hear it.

I want to share my whole story with you because it can show you how I went from being nothing more than your average defiant teenager to someone barely surviving on the streets. My story is the story of a girl who fell into such a deep and dark depression that she felt totally alone in the world, and how she discovered the power inside of herself to change.

I have faced the very worst rejection possible - the rejection of a child by her parents. I have seen my best friend murdered in cold blood. I have lived on the rockiest road you can imagine, and yet I found a way back to a healthy life.

I wish I could spare you the details, but you must read them for yourself if you are going to understand that anything, and I mean anything, is possible. Life is very difficult for everyone - even if we don't believe that's true - but it doesn't always have to be a struggle, and my story proves that. So, let's start at the beginning.

Chapter Two

A FATHER'S APPROVAL

"Esther, I just don't understand," my father said with a sigh, peering at me over the glasses at the end of his nose.

He always had this way of looking over the top of his glasses, even when he was sitting down and looking up at you! He always did this with his eyebrows raised, as if he were waiting for you to respond, but he really didn't want to hear anything you had to say.

I already knew there was nothing I could say that would make this situation okay, so I just looked back at him. Shaking his head, he flipped through the pages of my most recent report card and continued sighing.

"Biology…C-," he said and flipped to the next page.

"American History…D," he read. "Lydia got straight A's," he went on, but he said it as if it were some sort of question. When I didn't say anything, he said what I knew he was going to say all along:

"Why can't you be like your brother and your sisters?"

Yup…there it was.

The only question, the BIG question. The biggest question of them all, actually.

Why am I me and not identical to my siblings?

Why do I have to be myself and not another machine that says "yes, Poppa" and "yes, Mama" while getting straight A's?

I know that I am making them sound terrible, but in some ways, they are terrible. They knew right from wrong, fair from unfair, and yet they never treated me like they should. They also wondered why I was such a pain and didn't work as hard as they did.

Lydia is one year older than me. Our only brother, Daniel, is the oldest of us all. There are two more girls, both younger than me, but both identical to Lydia - they were both perfect too. Their names are Darline and Widelene.

"Even Widelene is getting high marks," my father just kept on saying, "and she is only in the second grade."

When he said this, I started to get angry. I was so tired of it all, but I didn't feel like getting into another of the no-win arguments with him and my mother about how I was such a disappointment. Instead, I just pointed to my report card and asked, "What was my pottery grade?"

I had done a ceramics class the first semester, and my art teacher said I would be a "natural" on the pottery wheel. I took the course and knew I had done okay. He hadn't even looked and flipped through the pages. He actually snorted when he read it.

"A B in pottery…what do you know, she knows how to play with mud!" he laughed.

I wanted to scream! Didn't he know how hard it was to make a perfect pot or plate on the wheel? It took me a few weeks just to get the clay on the wheel properly, and then the rest of the semester to master how to do the different shapes and the glazing. It was serious work, and my teacher didn't just hand out good grades because she was so nice. A lot of kids called her nasty names and said she was too uptight to be an artist, and that was why she had to teach instead of just living by making art.

I didn't agree. She was a perfectionist, for sure, someone who wanted everything done a certain way. But how was that different from our English teacher who knocked off points if you used a colon or semicolon wrong? Now *he* was uptight!

"What about my grades for chorus and band?" I asked. I already knew I got B's for both of those classes too.

"Yeah…I see, but are you going to sing and dance for a living?" he said.

I decided it was time to stop speaking. I did what I always did - I went silent. In fact, I began to zone out.

I would start by thinking about a song or a book, maybe even the spinning clay on the pottery wheel or a drawing I was working on, and soon it was as if I were there instead of standing in front of my father.

I would stay that way until he raised his voice and barked my name to bring me back to the conversation. From time to time, he used his hand on my face instead of just yelling at me, and I used to believe I deserved the smack because I was ignoring him.

Even then, I knew that my zoning out was just a coping mechanism. I had learned about it in my sociology class. I remember listening to our teacher start the lesson, and almost instantly, he had my attention.

"We are animals, but we are very complex animals," he said. "Our lives are also very complicated. We have social circles everywhere - at home, at work, at school and so on. Because our lives are complex, we are not always going to cope with things easily, and when we feel tense, stressed, or overwhelmed, we use coping mechanisms."

Stressed, I thought, *and overwhelmed… those are my middle names! Maybe I should get some of those coping mechanisms!* After all, it sounded like it might be good to have them.

My teacher described them using phrases like humor, problem-solving, exercise, and adjusting expectations. These all made sense. Find humor or look at something in a more positive way to cope with it. Look for the source of the problem or stress to cope with it, or just take a long run or swim and burn off the stress you feel.

How I wish I could have used any of those methods to deal with my problems! Instead, I would use unhealthy coping mechanisms like denial, self-blame, and venting, and when these bumped up against my depression, it was a recipe for disaster.

LEARNING TO COPE…OR NOT

My home life was one endless string of stressed-out and overwhelming moments. I could not please my father, my brother and sisters were flawless, and my mother just kept quiet while wearing a miserable look on her face. I felt like I must have been adopted, and I was so beaten down by all of their rejection, rejection, and more rejection.

There were so many times I wanted to scream, "Doesn't anyone in this house like me?"

I wasn't going to bother asking about love. We didn't use that word…ever. It was so weird when I would be with a friend who was on the phone with their mother or father, or even a brother or sister, and would say "love you" before hanging up. We never, ever said "I love you."

So, I just wondered whether any of them even liked me. It seemed as if they could hardly stand me. I was gross, lazy, and something that made them feel ashamed. They wanted nothing to do with me - even when I did my best.

Now, a few years after all of my troubles, I understand that I was feeling angry because I was being rejected. In fact, it was even worse than that.

My therapist has worked with me for a long time, and together we discovered that I just never had any relationship with my parents - even as a very small kid. My parents never let me feel protected or safe; they never showed me that adults could be trusted.

Though my mother was better than my father at accepting me and my behaviors, she always took my father's side and never challenged him.

So, as time passed, I began to feel unwanted and abandoned, but it got a lot worse when I became a teenager.

This was because my parents had never been there for me, and now, suddenly, they started to try to control me.

Instead of just sighing and saying, "You're not trying hard enough," they became my worst critics. They rejected everything - even my top grades in my favorite classes - and I felt no attachment to them. Soon, all I wanted was to get away - far away.

To cope, I started that zoning-out behavior as a way to get away from the mean words and unfair comments. And when I would get a smack for it, I blamed myself, telling myself it was what I deserved.

Sometimes, even that little bit of emotion and attention from my father made me happy.

Imagine…I was happy when he smacked me because it meant I was real, that he saw me and knew I was a real person! My therapist says that all kids, depressed or not, want attention from their parents, and sometimes they act out in bad ways, get negative attention (like yelling or slapping), and are happy about it.

I wanted their attention, but I also wanted them to accept me, to stop treating me like an outsider. I couldn't get that from them in a positive way (with good grades), so I was doing bad things to get them to look at me.

I didn't know it, but I was also already starting to look for a father figure by that time. I wanted someone who could be a good substitute for my father, but I didn't understand this about myself.

I didn't know I had this issue, which a lot of people jokingly call a "daddy issue." All that I knew was that I wanted his approval, but I also knew I couldn't get it. I was not Daniel, Lydia, Darline, or Widelene. I was just me - and I was not good enough.

But I knew I could be good enough in other ways and for other people, and that is when things started to go from bad to worse.

I had already designed my own coping mechanisms. These were my personal responses to the stress of living with parents who rejected me, and they were things I did out of desperation to feel better. My therapist explained that I was denying the issue, blaming myself for a lot of things, and venting too much to my friends.

The result was that I began to do things that made it all worse. Drinking, avoiding schoolwork, sleeping a lot, and doing things to get attention from men were just some of my ways of coping. You might already see that I was just running away from problems instead of solving them. I didn't see that. So, instead of getting better, things got worse, and this made me truly run away from home.

LEAVING HOME

While it was true that my family situation also made things worse, I began to make choices and mistakes that made it impossible to be happy at home.

I had total disapproval in my family life. My father disliked me and rejected me because I did not do well in school and behave the way he wanted his children to behave. I was creative and a bit messy. He liked us to be very tidy, organized, and practical. Sometimes, I argued or zoned out - and he really hated it when I did either of these things.

My mother would never speak out against my father's words or actions, and my brother and sisters believed I was trouble. They actually avoided me and kept me out of different conversations or activities. I don't think they did it to be mean. I think they did it because they did not want to see my father looking at them the way he looked at me. They wanted to keep his approval.

They abandoned their sister because they were afraid of our parents rejecting them!

In our household, Dad's approval was the only sort of love we could ever get from him. I don't blame my brother and sisters for rejecting me, because I understand the pressures they felt.

Today, I see that my reaction to those pressures is what caused me to make bad choices. How can I blame my family for bad choices when I made my own bad choices too?

So, I got angrier, sadder, and more distant and rebellious. My father just got angrier and soon was only speaking to me if he absolutely had to. My mother looked after us, but she was never one for sitting down and chatting as if we were individual people. My siblings were scared of me and kept me at a distance.

I began to feel invisible, and on the day that my report card came and my father refused to see my achievements, I decided it was time to go.

"What about my grades for chorus and band?" I had asked, attempting to show him that there were three decent grades on that report card in front of him.

"Yeah…I see, but are you going to sing and dance for a living?" he had said with a smirk.

I began to zone out, mentally drifting away. I was remembering just a day or two earlier when I was with some new friends, skipping school, and we were all dancing in someone's apartment. We had opened a bottle of vodka and were all pretty drunk. We were bouncing around, and I felt dizzy but also free…

SMACK!

My father had slapped my face to bring me back to reality.

"I said," he yelled into my face, "you can dance and sing on the street, but if you are living in this house, you will study real things, get good grades in all classes, and pay attention when your father is speaking."

My ears were ringing from his slap, and I was ready to cry but also wanted to scream with anger and rage. I could hear that my brother and sisters had stopped talking in the next room. The sound of my mother humming as she did something in the kitchen had stopped too.

Everyone was waiting, listening, but not coming to see whether they could help. Suddenly, I just felt empty. I was as silent inside as the house around me. There was not a peep from anyone, and inside of myself it was just as silent and empty.

I had no urge to argue or fight; I didn't feel like crying or screaming. I didn't see a point to doing anything. I didn't even put my hand to my face.

"Did you hear me?" he yelled.

"Yes," I answered, and turned and walked upstairs to my room.

Even as I lay down on my bed, I was wondering, *What is wrong with me?* I felt like I had run out of emotions. I felt helpless and hopeless and didn't think there was a point in trying to get his approval anymore. I had always understood that my parents had ideas about us kids and wanted us to do or be certain things. It was only part of the pressure all five of us felt.

I had these pressures too, but I also had something else going on inside of me. I was developing clinical depression. I did not know it then, though.

REJECTION AND DEPRESSION

Today, I can remember the way that I felt and how it made me act. I can see that if my parents had been better about things, they might have seen I was ill, but all they could see was that I was a failure (in their eyes).

So, instead of getting help, I got more and more criticism and rejection. This is worse than it might sound, because of my depression.

When people are truly depressed, they feel like no one understands them, that they are alone and hopeless, and that it will never change. Depression changes the chemistry in the brain, so it was not like I could just tell myself that the way I felt was wrong or say to myself, "Don't worry, it will get better," and believe that. I honestly saw no way that things could change.

Instead, my parents telling me I was unwanted and unloved, my sense of being rejected and alone, and the depression telling me all of those same things, well…it led to disaster after disaster.

MY CHOICES

After my father slapped my face, I went to my room and spent time lying on my bed looking back at the past few years. It seemed like everything had just kept getting worse and worse after I entered high school. My father's expectations and the endless pressures to be like my older brother and sister had become like a ton of weight on me.

I just knew in my heart that I would never get the same high grades. I would not get the smile of approval from my parents.

So, what did I do? I went out and got a smile of approval from all of the boys at school.

How? It started slowly.

First, I took the shirt I wore in my school uniform, and I trimmed it to make the neckline lower. In our family, most of the girls have big chests, and so I wanted to show off as soon as I started to develop. Cutting the neckline of the shirt let everyone see my chest and even the top edge of my bra. When a teacher was nearby, I would just close my coat or sweater over it.

Then, I started to roll up my skirt at the waist after I got on the bus. This made it shorter, and I wore it above my knees to show off my long, skinny legs. Teachers did catch me at this, and I got in trouble.

The second time I got caught changing my uniform, making the skirt too short and the shirt too low, they called my mother. She said she would get me new clothes that fit properly, and when I got home that day, she was waiting with three new uniforms and had taken all of the school clothes I had in my closet.

"I did not tell your father," she said. "But do this again, and I will have to explain why I am spending so much on your clothes."

That didn't stop me, and when I changed the new clothes, my father exploded. He yelled at me, telling me what a horrible person I was for ruining good clothes, and what a trashy girl I was to show off my body to the boys. "Do you want us to be ashamed? What about your sisters? Do you want the boys to think they are like you?"

He also said that I would have to start paying for new uniforms from the money I earned during the summer as a babysitter. Over the past three summers, I had saved up over a thousand dollars, but I didn't want him to take it for ugly uniforms. So, I stopped changing them.

I also started skipping school.

When I got in trouble for the uniforms, I got a lot of attention. There was a group of kids at school whom everyone knew as the rebels. They smoked, they skipped, they kissed and made out in front of people, and they did a lot more than that. Some said they did drugs, and everyone knew they were already having sex.

Getting in trouble got me their attention, and soon they were talking to me and asking me to hang out. This meant blowing off school and going to someone's house to drink, smoke, and get crazy.

By crazy, I mean pretty crazy. We would go as a group to a store, and one or two would steal something. It wasn't candy or cheap things either. It was stuff they could put online or take to a guy who gave us cash. I was nervous at first, but soon, I stopped caring. It was like I was becoming another person, and I liked that because I didn't like myself that much to begin with.

I liked fitting in for once. With them, I never heard anyone mention Lydia or Daniel. Teachers were always expecting me to be like them, and a lot of the other kids thought it was weird that I didn't act like my older siblings, but my new friends didn't care at all.

Especially the boys.

The boys said they liked my short skirts, and that I was "fierce." They smiled and laughed when I argued, smoked, drank, and skipped school. They thought I was cool because I got bad grades and didn't care, but what they really liked about me was that I was willing to have sex with some of them.

I won't lie - I wasn't just willing to do it; I was aggressive about it. I was the one that went after them, instead of making them chase me. I wanted all of the boys to like me more than they liked any other girl, and I knew that I could get that by having sex with them.

At least, that is what I believed then.

Today, I know it was a desperate thing that I did to get their approval, to fit in and get them to like me. I couldn't get my dad to approve of me, but these boys would really like me if I gave them what they wanted, and so I did.

Did it make me feel better? No. When I was with the boys, I did not feel happy or good about myself. Sometimes, I didn't even really like the boy; I just wanted to win his attention. The attention never lasted. After it was over, most of them were not interested in me anymore.

This made it hard to be good friends with the girls because they got mad at me or jealous. I thought I didn't care. I was so busy trying to make boys like me that I didn't care if the girls hated me for having sex with the boys they liked.

Soon, a lot of my new friends were not so happy to hang out with me. None of the boys were interested, and most of the girls were angry. They called me trouble or said I was into drama. I just got mad and blamed them for being like everyone else.

We didn't skip a lot of school as a group. Just days here or there. We didn't want to get caught. What we did do was lie to our parents about after-school stuff. We would all leave school and go to someone's house or to a spot we had at a local park, and we'd get into all kinds of trouble. Once things began to change between me and that group, though, they stopped telling me where they were going to meet up, and soon they were almost totally ignoring me.

I felt like I was being rejected all over again, and so I found new friends. These were older kids, most of them not even in school anymore. I met them hanging out with my crowd one day skipping school.

It was mostly a group of older guys who were selling stuff to my friends. They could get alcohol and drugs, and my friends were buying. I never used drugs. I saw how they made people lose total control, and I just never wanted to be that way.

I actually thought I was in control, though I know now that I wasn't. I drank a lot and smoked way too many cigarettes, but I avoided the drugs.

Once my school friends didn't seem to think I was cool anymore, I decided to hang out with the older group. The guys seemed to like me, and soon we were partying a lot - almost every day. This was towards the end of the semester, just a few weeks left to go, and so I didn't think it could make my grades any worse than they were. Actually, I knew I was going to fail most of my classes.

To get away with skipping so many days, I would wear my school uniform as if I was going to school, but keep some clothes hidden in my backpack. Then I would change somewhere on the street where one of them would pick me up, and we'd head somewhere to hang out all day.

Because I was in a different school than Daniel and Lydia, no one knew what I was doing…until the day my report card came and my parents could see that all of my grades were terrible except for art and music.

That day, my father smacked me hard, and I was a world away when he did it. I just couldn't hear his words anymore; I couldn't bear it.

I had disappeared into a daydream about partying with the guys, being drunk, and feeling almost nothing. I thought it was a good escape. My father's slap, and the way I sort of collapsed inside myself, made me want to run. It was the first time I had ever seriously thought about running away.

I decided that it was time, so I packed up some of my clothes. When everyone went to bed, I just left.

I went to find some of the guys I was hanging around with and asked whether I could stay with some of them. Only one of them offered me a place to stay but said I would have to earn it. He laughed about that, and the other guys did too. I didn't know what he meant, and so he explained.

If I wanted a place to stay, I could use one room he had, but I would have to be one of his "girls."

"Do you mean that I have to have sex with you if I want the room?" I asked.

He laughed. "Are you stupid? No, I don't wanna be with you. You got to do that with the guys ready to pay you for it."

I thought I was going to be sick. These were my friends. I thought these guys liked me. They didn't. They thought I was a joke, and the only way they would let me be around them was if I were a prostitute out on the street, earning money for them to use to party.

"I thought you liked me!" I yelled at them.

"Oh," one said, "we like you, baby, but everyone's got to earn their way."

I just ran. I picked up my pack and ran. I had no idea where I was going or what I was doing, but I didn't want to be near them. I stopped when I reached a park near my parents' house.

I wondered whether I could go home, and then I remembered my father's face, the sound of the slap, and how he seemed to really hate me. I realized that all of my skipping was probably going to come out and that it would only make things worse.

"If you thought your home life was crap before," I said to myself, "it will be ten times worse if you go back right now."

I was so alone. Then, one of the boys I used to hang out with came walking up to me. He sat on the curb next to me and asked where I had been hanging out lately. I told him I didn't want to talk. He poked my bag and asked, "You going on a trip or something?"

I forgot I had most of my clothes all jammed into the huge pack. "It's nothing," I said, trying to avoid a conversation.

"Look," he said, "I know things weren't so good for you at home, and I think you bailed."

He waited, but I didn't answer.

"I got a place you can crash at if you want," he offered.

"Yeah," I laughed. "And what do I have to do to get that place to crash?"

I was already starting to realize that life on the streets might mean no life at all. It might mean doing crazy things for money, food, or a place to stay.

"Nothing," he said. "It ain't an actual house or anything, just an old trailer nobody is using. I stay there, and you can have one of the rooms if you want…that's all."

His name was Denver. I didn't know whether that was his real name or a made-up one. Maybe he had come from the city of Denver. I didn't ask that day, but I looked at him and saw he looked as innocent as I felt. He didn't have cold, hard eyes like the guy who had just offered me a home in exchange for work as a prostitute. His were big and brown, and had eyelashes so thick and long that most women would be jealous of them.

"Okay," I said. "That would be great."

It was not as bad as I had imagined. Someone had once lived in the trailer, but now it didn't have any electricity or water. The roof didn't leak, though; the doors and windows were all there; and as far as I could see, there were no mice or rats. Denver had a padlock on the main door and used his key to pop it open.

I had some money from my savings, so we went to The Salvation Army and got some stuff for me to sleep on - a sleeping bag, an old pillow, and some big cushions. It was kind of cool, like camping out. Because I lived in California, I knew we didn't have to worry about cold winter nights, so that trailer was a pretty amazing thing to have.

Over the next few days, Denver and I became real friends. We worked to make the trailer cleaner, and we even set up a sort of alarm by stringing old cans around the outside. If anyone came close, they would make the cans rattle, and we would know that someone was poking around our "house."

I told him I had a little money and that we could use it for food and stuff. A thousand dollars sounds like a lot, especially when you don't have to pay for anything but food, water, and some supplies.

My money lasted us for around three months.

I knew it was going to run out, but one of my coping mechanisms was denial. I just kept thinking that we would find a way or get by somehow.

Then, I would go to one of the guys we knew who could sell us alcohol, and I would spend some of that precious money on a bottle of something so we could just drink all night.

Getting drunk was not a good solution, and it only made my depression symptoms worse. I didn't know I was someone with depression. I just knew that I was always sad or angry, that nothing was fun, that I didn't see any point in trying to do anything else in my life, and that I was worthless.

I slept as much as I could, had constant headaches, lost a lot of weight, didn't take any baths or showers, and was thinking a lot about dying. I wasn't suicidal, but I just wondered whether it wouldn't be better if I were just to die in my sleep or something.

Then, the day came when we needed food but had no money. Because both of us were under the age of 18 (my birthday was still months in the future), we didn't want to ask for help because we knew social services would send us home or to some county facility.

So, we did what we thought was the best solution. We stole what we needed. Neither one of us was very good at it, but we were able to hit different spots each day, stealing a few cans of food or some package of snacks.

It was when I tried to steal a bottle of vodka that I got caught.

A MOTHER'S LOVE

"No," Denver said, pulling at my sleeve. "Not a packy."

He meant a package store, a place that only sold liquor, beer and lottery tickets, and it was my target for that night. I had not had a drink for a week, and I really wanted to get drunk. I wasn't thinking. All I could see was the bottle coming towards my mouth and the buzz that would help me forget about my parents, my life, and the fact that I felt so alone in the world.

I wanted that bottle, and I was going to get it.

Of course, that didn't mean I was super good at stealing, and though I looked older than my 17 years, the clerk behind the counter made a point of watching me. I didn't think about the security cameras; I just thought, *I can't see him, so he can't see me.*

The reality was that he was watching me the entire time on the TV behind the counter! He had already called the cops before I had made my way towards the front. He stopped me as I was heading to the door.

"Excuse me, please, miss," he said politely. "I think you forgot something." He nodded toward the aisle where I had been "shopping."

I looked down the aisle and said, "No, I didn't leave anything there," and shook my head.

He smiled again. "I didn't say you forgot something in the aisle."

I was confused. "I'm not sure what you mean," I said.

"Ah," he said. "Okay. What I mean is this…you forgot to pay for that bottle in your sleeve."

My heart might have stopped. I felt all of the blood rush up into my face. It actually felt like my face was swelling, and I could hear blood whooshing in my ears. I was caught!

I thought for one second and glanced around. There was no one else in the store, so I thought I could bolt out the door. When I turned to look at the clerk, he was no longer smiling.

I turned to run, and as I did, I saw the police car parked outside and the police officers already heading towards the store.

I won't explain how embarrassing and scary it was to be arrested without any sort of identification while trying to steal alcohol. The cops brought me to the station and took fingerprints. I decided it would be best just to tell them who I was. I didn't give them any other information.

They put me in a cell by myself, because I was a minor, and told me to just stay calm. They were going to have someone from the county come to speak with me. About three hours went by, and then I was brought to a room where a very overweight man in a suit sat waiting for me.

"Esther," he said, "I am Jock Daniels, an attorney hired by your mother."

I was speechless. My mother! My mother had an attorney?

"She has paid me to come here today and to handle your arrest...okay?"

I could only nod. I had no idea what was happening here.

"Okay," he continued. "So, because it is your first time as a shoplifter, the juvenile court has opted to just release you into the care of your parent or guardian."

Great, I thought with a huge wave of fear and dread. *This guy is about to send me to my parents!*

"Your mother came to me to find out what would happen here today, and I explained that I thought you would probably be released to her care." He was watching my face really closely as he spoke. "She asked if there was some way you could be released without her being responsible for you after that."

"What?" I said in a mumble. I was stunned. I couldn't believe my mother didn't want anything to do with me.

"I told her it would be impossible, but she decided to have me handle everything and to just let you know that she paid your bail," he said. "It's unusual, and the court would frown on this, but it is what has happened."

"Wait," I said, struggling to understand this. "My mother knows I was arrested, paid my bail, but she doesn't want anything to do with me now? I can't go home?"

He began fumbling with folders and paperwork, forcing things into his briefcase.

"Well," he said, "it wasn't put to me like that."

"Okay," I said, beginning to feel enormously sad and just as enormously angry. "How did she put it?"

"The arresting officer told her that you looked like you might be living on the street, and that it would be good if your family stepped up," he said, "but I think that may have upset your mother."

Upset *her*? Her! I had nothing to say about that. I was on the street, struggling and starving. No one had come to find me, and when I *was* found, alive and well, she wanted nothing to do with me. Was I nothing more than a problem to her?

"She told him that she was stepping up enough by paying the bail," he said, "and then told me that was all she and the rest of your family were prepared to do."

It felt like a sliver of ice had just slipped into my heart when he finished speaking. I felt cold, even though it was a hot day outside.

"What about my father?" I asked.

He just shook his head and said, "I didn't hear anything about your father."

"Does he know?" I asked.

"Honestly, Esther," he said with a sigh, "I have no idea…why don't you use this as a reason to get in touch with them? It sounds like you all have some issues to resolve."

He was so, so right, about all of us. I wish I could have really heard him when he said, "you all have some issues." He was seeing it so clearly. I was not the problem; my entire family was having issues.

THE MEANING OF HEARTBREAK

We all have some issues to resolve…that kept repeating in my head as I walked back to the trailer from the jail. Denver was so glad to see me, and that made me feel a lot better, but it didn't stop the endless loop of thoughts rattling in my brain.

They know I am out on the streets…

They won't come to look for me...

They sincerely don't care...

I didn't even realize that I was hoping they would come look for me, but now I know that I wanted them to reach out…

Why won't they reach out?

Why don't they care?

Then, it would begin again…*My God…they know I live on the streets! They won't come to look for me*…and on and on.

Today, I have spent many hours in therapy, and one of the things I know I must do to reduce the risk of depression is to avoid isolation.

Isolation can take many forms. I might keep myself all alone in a room, and that is isolation. I might refuse to answer phone messages or stay in touch with friends and family. That is isolation. I might spend too many hours online when I have friends nearby, and this too is isolation.

Keeping myself stuck in that loop of thoughts about my family…that was another kind of isolation as well.

What I should have done was to find an adult with whom to speak about what was happening to me, or to ask for help when I was with the police. I should not have isolated myself with just one friend who was also isolating himself from the world.

I did none of those things. Instead, I got angry. I got angry, and I held on to that anger like it was the only thing I had. I felt something inside of myself becoming cold and hard. I felt some sort of wall going up between me and any thoughts about my parents, friends, or anyone besides Denver.

I told Denver that it was just the two of us now and that we would have to do whatever it took to get by and stay alive on the streets.

"What're we gonna do?" he asked with those gentle eyes staring right at me.

"Don't worry," I said. "I have an idea."

Chapter Three

TRULY ALONE

My idea was this: Denver could continue to do his street stuff, stealing and selling. I would go back to my "friends" and accept their offer. I would work for them as one of their girls, but for cash, not for a roof over my head.

"No," Denver said. "I don't like it. It is stupid and dangerous."

"It is the only answer I have!" I argued.

Really, it was the only answer I wanted to have.

At that time, I felt like I was the most unloved, worthless thing that ever existed. My parents didn't care whether I lived or died. They just didn't want me to be a problem anymore. I had no money, no home, and no job, and what I deserved was the life in front of me. That was what I truly believed.

In reality, I wasn't thinking straight. I was angry and sad, and my depression made me feel helpless. I believed I was worthless and wrong or bad. I thought that living in that dirty old trailer, stealing and working as a prostitute, was where I belonged.

It was partly because of the bad things my father said to me as I grew up, telling me I was never good enough. It was also the chemicals inside of my brain, holding me in that dark place where I just couldn't see or hear anything else.

Denver told me about living in foster care and group homes, and how people told him to work with the system to have a better way of life. He said that he'd been in more than ten homes while growing up, but he was always running away because the people in foster homes or group homes were mean, or they didn't treat you well.

"They hated us," he said one night as we tried to figure out what to do. "I can't go back to living like that…anyway, I think I'm too old for it."

"What do they do for people our age?" I asked him.

"Do?" he said, laughing. "I don't think they will do anything. We're both almost 18, and that means we are adults."

I realized what he was saying. We were on our own. I know today that we were both wrong. There was help in social services and outreach centers, and even though I don't think my parents would have helped, I could have always just called them too.

Instead, we decided to stick with my crazy plan. Denver would do the same street stuff he'd done for years: shoplifting, begging for change, and even selling drugs if he had a chance. I would go to work for that guy I had once thought was a friend.

THE DARK PATH

To say that working as a prostitute is like being a slave, for a teenage girl, is accurate. To say that I lived in a state of denial is true too. I felt like while my body was wherever it might be, my mind was far, far away.

For the next six months, I belonged to someone else. My old "friend" was named Angel, but he was definitely not like his name - he was no angel.

He decided when I worked, where I worked, and for how long I worked. He got almost every penny, and when I argued with him the first time, he took me to an alley and beat me up so bad I could hardly stand up afterward.

I learned not to challenge him, and some of the other girls I knew warned me that Angel was one of the worst on the streets. I heard he may have even killed one of the other girls.

I never challenged Angel, but I did have to be street tough with the men who stopped and paid me for my services. Being with strange men and letting them do what they wanted made me cold. My therapist uses the word "detached." I had to disconnect from myself to be able to do what I did.

I don't like remembering that time in my life, even though it lasted only half a year. Angel would take me to the place he wanted me to work. Sometimes it was a street, and sometimes it was a hotel. He told me what to say and what to do, and even taught me how to avoid being arrested if I was accidentally with a cop. If I used the right words and behaved in a certain way, I couldn't be accused of being a prostitute or get arrested.

I hated it, every minute of it, and even though I did get a tiny bit of money, I knew I couldn't keep living this way. Eventually, I would get hurt or sick.

Denver asked me what I would do if I became pregnant. I know it sounds crazy, but I didn't ever think about what I would do if that happened!

Another thing I never ever considered was being picked up by someone I knew - and then it happened.

I won't ever forget it. It was a chilly night, and none of us wanted to be out on the corner looking for work. A pretty nice sedan pulled up to the curb in front of me, and I was the one who headed to the window.

I spoke to the driver, and he let me get in the car. We drove off, but before I could say another word, the guy pulled to the curb up a few blocks and turned the lights on inside the car.

I was drunk and couldn't see clearly because my eyes were still getting used to the light, but I heard the guy sigh deeply, and then he started to speak.

"Esther," he said like my name was a bad thing. "I passed by you a few times in the past few weeks, and I thought it was you. I wasn't sure until tonight. "

That's when I recognized the smell. One of my dad's best friends is a man named Jacob, and he always wears a strongly scented cologne. He buys it in Haiti, where he grew up with my father, and I remembered that smell along with the sound of his voice.

I couldn't look at him.

"Girl," he said sounding angry, "isn't it enough that you shamed your family by running away? Now, you put yourself out here on the streets?"

I still couldn't look at him. I suddenly felt dirty. Not just dirty because of the job I did, but dirty because I wasn't bathing, wasn't thinking, and was living like a slave. Dirty because all of the nastiness I thought I had run away from was suddenly washing all over me again.

I thought I was free of that at least, but suddenly here it was again.

"I'm here to tell you," he said with a quieter voice, "you can't go on like this. It won't end good. You will bring even worse shame on your family if you die on the streets like a filthy dog."

My thoughts were raging as I listened to him.

After all, my parents had said they didn't want anything to do with me and paid a lawyer to deal with me. Yet this man was here telling me that I shouldn't make them more ashamed of me by living on the streets.

Was I supposed to just become invisible or stop existing? I didn't understand!

I ran away to escape these feelings, and even though I lived in a dirty shack and was selling myself to survive, I still had to hear that my parents didn't want to deal with me! I still had to feel everything I ran away from.

I wasn't ready to feel it, deal with it, or do anything about it. I wanted to just be left alone. What was the point of even arguing with this guy, this friend of my father's?

He didn't want to hear the truth. He just wanted me to agree and behave the way he thought I should. Just like my father and the guy I worked for, he didn't want to hear a thing out of me; I was just to do my job and shut up.

I didn't exist, and the worst part about it all was that I was starting to believe that to be the truth. I was beginning to feel like I didn't exist at all, and if I didn't exist, what was the reason to even continue living?

I couldn't escape my parents or their opinions about me. I had gone so low that I was never going to be able to deal with them again. Why continue? I was so tired.

I started thinking about the things that men had been doing to me, and how they had no respect for me as a human being. I also started to think that this man was treating me the same way - like I wasn't a human being with feelings.

I began to see myself in the same way. In that moment, sitting in that car, with all of those thoughts and ideas swirling in my head, the one clear thought I had was this:

I hate myself.

And yet, something else had happened in that moment too. That sliver of ice that had slipped into my heart when I heard that lawyer tell me that my parents really did not want anything to do with me, it had started to melt.

I want you to understand this, because it is so important. In that moment, sitting in the car and hearing my father's friend tell me that my family was ashamed of me for running way, I began to feel again.

I hadn't really felt anything for a while. It was like there was a tiny flame inside of me that began to melt that ice where my heart lived. It was like a small voice said, "Hey there…what's going on? You are alive…alive and awake! C'mon now…wake up."

It wasn't a big voice or a big fire; it wasn't enough to make me think clearly and make huge changes right then and there. But it was enough to help me turn to that man and fight back a bit.

"Shame? My parents should feel shame for being so cruel and cold that their child would have to run away from them to survive."

Jacob stared at me. I couldn't tell what he was thinking…and I didn't care.

"I am ashamed, yes, I am. But, I am also glad to be far away from them and their hard words and hard hearts. They cannot feel ashamed, Jacob, because they can't feel anything."

I got out of the car, slammed the door, and headed home. At least, I tried to head home…

Chapter Four

FRIENDSHIP

I was not just walking home; I was stomping home. I was mumbling angry words about Jacob, my parents, my brother and sisters, and about life as I trudged along the streets and through the park. I was angry, and it felt good. I realized I had been sort of sleepwalking through the past few months.

I stopped as I passed a reflection of myself in a large store window. I could see that I was barely recognizable. My hair was matted and dull, I was skinnier than I had ever been, my clothes were dirty, and I just looked awful. I couldn't imagine how I smelled.

I saw in that moment that I was going to have to change, but not for my parents and not for anyone else. For me. I wanted to be better than a dirty girl living a dirty life on the streets. I didn't want to hate myself.

The store I was standing in front of sold used electronics. All of the TVs were on, and a night news show was running. I saw the date and time in the corner of the screen and realized it was only three days until my 18th birthday. In three days, I was going to be an adult.

I thought to myself, *It's time to start growing up and becoming an adult.*

I wasn't sure how to do that, but I did know that the very first thing I needed to do was to get a different job. Sooner or later, my "work" was going to get me seriously hurt, sick with some horrible disease, or even killed.

I decided that I was going to go home and talk to Denver about all of this. I needed a friend to listen, and he was my very best friend.

Yes, you could say he was my only friend, but he was also the best friend I had ever had. He understood how it felt to be rejected by your own mother and father.

He understood what it felt like to never fit in anywhere. What I also see now, as I look back, is that Denver also struggled with serious depression too. We both felt and thought the same way, and when we talked to one another all of those nights in our little trailer, we were finally able to tell someone else about our feelings, and know that the other person understood it.

I mean, Denver really understood that I saw myself as weak, no good, and ashamed. I had to be so hard and fierce living on the streets, but with Denver, I was my real self. I didn't need some smart remark or nasty words. I could just be me.

It wasn't like we had all kinds of heart-to-heart talks, but he really understood me. He never tried to fix me; he just listened. He was such a great listener.

So, I wanted to tell him what had happened, and how I wanted to start making some changes. I turned to cut back through the park and then make my way to our trailer, but Angel was waiting at the next corner.

He saw me and strolled up to me. "What's up?" he said. It was not going to be a friendly chat.

I struggled to find the words.

I wanted to just say "I quit" but knew that he would not appreciate that, and so I said, "I needed to talk to you."

Angel shook his head and said, "Naw…naw…that ain't how it works, honey." I knew he was angry. "When I need to talk, we talk. Otherwise, I don't wanna hear it. You got me?"

He put his arm over my shoulder and I could tell he was trying to make everyone think we were having a good conversation, a happy and lighthearted one.

"Angel," I said, and I could hear the fear in my voice. "Listen, I…I can't do this anymore…okay?"

He didn't speak, but I heard him laugh through his nose, like a snort.

"I don't want to make trouble," I said, "but I gotta move on…alright?"

We had been walking while we were talking, and I saw we were now close to an alley. He kept on walking, and then we were inside the alley. I remember him hitting me hard, and maybe one or two other hits, but that's all.

I woke up alone in the alley. It was still nighttime, and the sounds of the street were still busy and loud. I had probably been out for just a few minutes, maybe a bit more. I knew he had broken a rib or something, and I knew he'd hit me hard in the face. I didn't want to see what I looked like.

I got to my hands and knees, and then slowly stood up, leaning on the wall to be safe. When my head was clear, I walked out of the alley and into the park. It took me a long time, but I made it home.

Denver was not home when I got there, so I went into my area and just went to sleep. I didn't care whether I woke up, and I didn't even feel like getting help from a doctor. I was just ready to sleep and sleep.

When I woke up, it was morning. I squinted in the light and sat up. Denver was reading an old newspaper and eating cereal out of the box. For a minute, I didn't remember the night before.

"Hey," I said and sat up, rubbing my hand against my eye. The pain was horrible, and I must have made a noise because Denver stopped reading to look at me.

"Oh man!" he yelled and came running over. "What happened?" he asked.

He was staring at my right eye, and I realized that must have been where Angel hit me so hard.

It was tough to think of the words I wanted to say. I felt like crying because of the beating, but I almost didn't care about it because I had already decided that I was done living this street life. Soon, we were going to be free of it. I didn't know how, but at least I knew that I was ready to get out.

I wasn't convinced that it would work. I still felt like I was the world's biggest loser and failure, but at the same time, something inside of me was saying, "Do this...you have got to do this."

So, I explained the best that I could. I told him about my father's friend and how unfair it felt to hear all of that garbage I had run away from. I told him how hard it was to hear those same things - I was an embarrassment, I was no good, and all the rest - even though I wasn't even around them anymore!

I knew Denver understood it all. He understood that I was sad and angry because they hadn't ever come looking for me, but I still couldn't escape their words.

He knew what I knew - I would never escape them living the way I lived. In fact, I was living in a way that fit with their ideas about me.

I was living in a shabby place, leading a second-rate life, and I was not doing my best. I was not trying. These were things they told me about myself, and I was making them true!

Then, I told him about Angel. I told him how he had beaten me and left me in the alley when I told him I wasn't going to work for him anymore. I told him that we would probably have to leave town or find a new place if we were going to get away from Angel.

Angel and his friends knew where we lived - everyone did really. No one bothered us, we were out of the way in a shack, so no one cared. But I thought we might be in trouble because of what I had done.

"Let's get out tomorrow," he said. "We'll pack up a few things today, I can get some money in the afternoon, and then we'll go."

"Where?" I asked, worried.

He smiled at me and said, "Wherever we want."

I wish it could have been that easy.

LOSS

I spent the day trying to feel better, packing up the few things we had, and saying goodbye to that happy little shack of ours. We agreed to meet at his pawnbroker's, where he could sell a few things for cash. Depending on what we made, we could take a bus or even a train to somewhere new.

I decided to clean up and went to the bus station to use its bathrooms. I had one or two decent and somewhat clean outfits, so I changed into a nice dress and some flip flops after I had washed up.

I brushed my hair and looked almost like my old self again. I know my face looked bad, but I knew I could tell people I had a bike accident or was in a car accident and hit my face. It looked just like I had anyway!

I went down the block to meet up with Denver before we were going to head to the broker. I had my pack, so it did look like I was going somewhere. I saw Denver about a block up the street, and I was looking around when I realized that Angel and his crew were headed towards me from the other way.

Angel actually hadn't seen me yet, so I turned to walk towards Denver. I was going as fast as I could, and I bumped into one or two people as I walked up the sidewalk. I decided to cross the street to be on the same side as Denver and as far away from Angel as possible.

I ran when there was a gap in traffic and kept on trotting along the sidewalk, trying to get far away from the danger behind me.

"Hold on for a second," I heard someone say close to me.

I didn't want to turn around or stop.

I kept going as fast as I could. Denver was now less than 25 feet away. He had a funny look on his face, and then he sort of jogged towards me.

"Hold on..." he yelled.

"Miss," the voice said again, and I felt a hand on my shoulder.

I turned and looked at a police officer. He was pretty young and was sweating. The day wasn't so hot, but maybe it was all of his gear.

"I said to hold on," he said angrily.

"Sorry," I said, and swiveled my head to see whether Denver was nearby. He had just caught up to me, and when I glanced across the street, I didn't see Angel or his pals.

"Is there a problem?" Denver asked.

"There wasn't," the cop said, "until you decided to run up in my face."

Denver took a step back, and I sort of stumbled away from the cop too.

"Hold on," I said, "he didn't mean to get in your face. He's..." But I didn't get to finish.

"Why did you run across the street when I came out of that store?" he asked me, and pointed back from where I had crossed the street.

"Sorry?" I said. I hadn't seen anything except Angel and a gang of guys walking towards me. The cop was probably there too, but I never saw him. However, I now knew why Angel disappeared so fast.

"You ran away from me," he said. "Why?"

"No, Officer," Denver said, "She didn't...she wasn't...it was another guy."

"I think you need to stand over there," he said to Denver and pointed to where he wanted him to go.

"No," Denver argued, "no, I just want to..."

The cop stopped pointing and angrily grabbed him, then shoved him away from us. "I am not talking to you!"

That's when I saw the other cop getting out of the car and rushing up. By the time he got to us, the first one had Denver in some sort of chokehold, and was telling him to get down. To this day, I am still not sure why Denver, who was always so calm, started to freak out. He was waving around his arms and fighting, and the other cop was trying to grab his hands.

I noticed that the one holding him around the neck had taken out his gun. I screamed, and Denver fought more. Then he reached into his pocket. I don't know what he was going to do, but one of the cops said, "Gun!" and they both got in tight on him.

I didn't see what happened, but I heard it. It was the sound of the trigger being pulled… twice.

They didn't step back, but Denver fell down with his whole weight on the ground. At first I told myself he'd passed out. Then I saw his face, and I knew what had happened. They'd killed him.

It was chaos. Other cops came out of nowhere, and soon I was alone in a sea of police and emergency people. They took Denver away in an ambulance, even though it was obvious that he was dead.

I sat, numb, on the ground. They had put me in handcuffs and were going to take me into the station to be questioned. When we got there, they put me in a room where I waited for a long time. Finally, an officer came in and told me that Denver had a whole bunch of stolen jewelry on him when he died.

Did I know where it came from?

I just shook my head. I didn't know anything. I even struggled to remember my name.

They asked a lot of questions about the two of us, and then about the "incident." They were trying to get me to say things, but I just didn't feel like talking. They'd killed my only real friend, and they'd done it in blind panic and cold blood. He was an 18-year-old kid who had nothing more than some gold chains in his pocket. No knife, no gun.

Maybe it is because we were two black street kids, maybe not. Maybe it was because I accidentally ran when that cop came out of a store. Maybe it was because the cop was young and scared. Maybe it was because Denver came running up to us and put his hand in his pocket.

I'll never know. What I will always remember is that he listened, that he was gentle and kind to me, and that he understood what it meant to be so alone that you wanted to die because of it.

In that moment, I sincerely wanted to die. Here, I had decided to change things. I had confronted Angel and told him I was done selling myself. I had forced Denver to give up the safe (but shabby) life he had been living and run away with me. Because of it, he got killed. All I had wanted to do was make a better life for the two of us, and even then, it seemed like I was doomed to spend the rest of my days on the streets. Even my escape plan blew up in my face.

THE STILL, SMALL VOICE

They kept me there answering all kinds of questions, but I didn't give them much information to work with. They brought me a sandwich and a soda. I wasn't hungry.

Then, suddenly, it was like there was a tiny voice inside of me: "Do you realize you have a chance here?"

That thought actually made me sort of sit up fast, like it came from nowhere. During the previous hours, I felt like I was living in the center of a black hole in the middle of a faraway universe. I was in a place so cold, lost, and remote that nothing could reach me.

And then that voice sort of echoed into my head. A chance? Here, in this room there was a chance? Yes, there was. Denver and I had been trying to leave. We had walked out of the trailer and into the streets; we had been heading away from trouble and towards some sort of future. It was just me and him against the world.

Now, it was just me...or was it? Wasn't the world still there? Wasn't I still there? I was sitting here with a policeman who could also help me escape Angel, the streets, and this way of life...I just had to ask for it.

I had to stop being angry and proud and ask for his help.

"What's the worst that could happen?" that voice said to me.

I thought about it for a second...it took only one second to make up my mind. The cop sitting across from me was just jotting notes on his paperwork.

"My name is Esther Santos," I said. He looked at me, surprised. "I turn 18 two days from now," I finished.

He said, "Hold up...you're only 17?"

I nodded my head yes.

"Okay," he said. "Gimme a minute."

He got on his phone and opened the door to call someone. Soon a person from Social Services was with me, and I told them my story. I said that I was a minor, but that I also knew I could ask them for help, regardless of whether my parents were going to approve. The man said that I could, but that I would not get a foster home option because of my age.

I told him I would work with him in whatever way necessary to get a safe place to live. I explained about Angel and my "work" on the streets. I told him I wanted to see a doctor to be sure I was not ill or severely injured by that beating. I told him that I was ready to change everything, and that I had already started when Denver was killed.

I told him how tired I was and that I just wanted to stop and recover something of myself. I didn't want any part of my old life - even the life with my parents. I wanted something that let me be myself.

Conclusion

ME TODAY... RETURNING TO THE LIGHT

Is that what I got? Yes and no.

I didn't get to just stop and rest. I had to go from the jail to a transitional living program. It was a place where runaways stay and get access to all kinds of programs. I had my pack with its few belongings. I was given a bed in a room with three other girls. It wasn't easy because I had to be street tough with some of them, and some of them were not ready to transition off the streets.

The good news was that I was able to get into counseling almost right away. The third day in my transitional living program (TLP), the social worker from the courthouse got in touch. He had arranged for me to visit a therapist for outpatient treatment.

During my first visit, we didn't really dig into too much, but she did get me to tell her the story of my parents, about running away, and how I ended up on the streets. Pretty quickly, she created a treatment plan that included talk therapy and some medications for depression.

This was when I learned that I was clinically depressed and that I was dealing with a lot of stress and pressure from my family life. To deal with this, my therapist had me join a group therapy session each week, and we worked on building my social connections.

"You've been isolating yourself in many ways, Esther," she said. "We've got to work to overcome that."

At first, I was volunteering in the TLP, helping in the kitchen and doing some cleaning. I was able to get a job in a fast-food place, and then an amazing job in a gourmet coffee chain. In about a year's time, I had gotten my GED (high school diploma) - and even better, I was working at getting into art school.

Today, I have gone through so many hours of therapy that I have lost count. I need it because I still don't always choose the right coping mechanisms. I take a lot less medication because we figured out a lot of the reasons for my depression.

I still don't have a relationship with my parents, but my brother and sisters did find me and get in touch. It was amazing to hear from them, and when I was invited to show one of my drawings in a city art show, they came to see my work! We see one another a few times each month for a pizza or a coffee, but for now that is all I can handle.

I have to be very careful when I deal with men. I am still, unfortunately, dealing with my wish for a father to love me, and so I sometimes make bad choices in boyfriends or treat male friends like boyfriends.

Maybe I will always have to deal with that, and that's okay. The good news is that I am finally aware of it and don't let things get out of control or upset me.

I am also still struggling with rejection and abandonment issues, but my therapy has helped me to learn some incredible ways for dealing with these things. For instance, everyone gets rejected! Before therapy, I just couldn't understand that supermodels and mega movie stars, sports heroes, and the world's best writers all face rejection. Why should I think I shouldn't deal with it?

The best thing I learned along the journey is that everyone has issues like this. It is not just the weird, odd, different, or "wrong" people, because there is no such thing as weird, odd, different, or wrong. We are all unique - that's it.

My parents refused to see things like that. They wanted all five kids to be the same, behave the same, and work like a smooth machine. Life doesn't work that way. It is a beautiful mess, but it is not always a messy, rocky, and impossible road. Sometimes it is a smooth and beautiful one.

I don't use the "blame game" anymore. That is what my therapist calls it when someone wants to blame themselves or their family for depression. It is not my fault I became depressed, and it is not my parents' fault that I ran away and had such a horrible time. There is no one to blame for depression, but with courage and therapy, I have learned how to react better to my depression, and how to make healthy choices.

One of the healthiest choices of all was to listen to that still and small voice inside of myself. It told me to wake up, it warned me that I was throwing away an opportunity to recover myself, and it made sure I saved myself. It is the same voice that helps me to express myself every day too.

After all, part of my recovery has been my art. Before, I was unable to really enjoy my artistic side, and now, it is the center of my life. I am able to use my imagination and my creativity as much as I need. Being unable to do that when I was younger actually made me depressed. It was part of the reason I suffered from depression!

Now, I do ceramics, draw, paint, sew, and listen to music all of the time. I learned how to do special fabric dyeing techniques, and I love to experiment in the kitchen.

Would it surprise you to learn that I also make sure to exercise for at least 30 minutes each day, eat a super-healthy diet, and always look for the positive and good things? This is just part of my recovery, and they are things I will have to make sure to do every day for the rest of my life. I have learned to identify the troubles in my life, but I no longer dwell on them. Instead, I spent time in therapy learning about the things that trigger my depression, and now that I know what makes me sad or angry, I know how to talk about my feelings and then return to the positive things in life.

I now know when to ask for help and exactly whom to ask. I have created a social circle around myself that allows me to share my thoughts and feelings in healthy ways. I don't have my original family back, but I have created a forever family with my friends and co-workers, as well as my siblings. I have online support groups, and I do a lot of reading about depression and family issues.

When you have depression, as I do, you need to be sure you are keeping it as under control as much as possible. I use several steps to manage it and remain healthy, happy and successful.

What are those steps?

- Talk to an adult if you are feeling depressed or rejected, or even if you just suspect you are depressed. It can be a parent, teacher, or even a gym coach, dance instructor…the point is to pick an adult and tell him or her about your strong feelings.
- Be ready to ask for help and to take the help that is offered.
- Learn what might set you off in depression or your struggles; face it by talking about it, writing about it, or both. Then focus on the positive and move past it.
- Exercise daily, express yourself in some way, and follow a good diet.
- Try to always think positive!

Those are "Esther's Tips for a Healthy Life."

I even have my own little studio apartment now, and each day I look around and wonder at how nice my life is turning out. Sometimes, I think about Denver. It was hard to remember him as I told this story, but instead of dwelling on the sad stuff, I remember what a good person he was, how his laugh was so big, and how he could listen and really hear what you said. I try to do that for other people too, and it helps me to feel better and even understand myself more.

Anyone who has ever dealt with depression should know that there are millions of people just like you, and that there is nothing wrong or shameful about it. Help is ready and waiting, and all you have to do is ask for it, or pick up the phone and call your nearest crisis hotline.

I can guarantee that just one step towards the light, towards getting better, is enough to keep you moving that way. I had to suffer a lot before I realized that life is not always so miserable, tough, and cold and that I just had to ask one person for help to get it.

Because I was living with depression, and because that depression caused me to make a few bad choices, I had a hard time finding a healthier path. Homelessness, prostitution, alcohol abuse…these were some of the challenges I encountered along with my depression, and if I can make my way to a better life, you can too.

It doesn't matter whether you are white or black, rich or poor, ugly or gorgeous, smart or of average intelligence…you can have depression. You can just as easily find yourself in the same place I found myself. I came from smart parents with college educations, I had four siblings who were the best students in their classes, and we lived in a very comfortable home. Yet there I was, a homeless prostitute before the age of 18.

Yes, it was depression, stress, abandonment, yearning for my father's love and approval, and so many other factors that brought me to the lowest point, but I got back up again.

I shared my story of sinking down into the darkest place imaginable to show you that you can return back to life and the light. I have, and though I need to always be aware of myself, that is the story of life. No one should just blunder through without stopping to examine their life, their feelings, their thoughts, and all the rest.

I have my scars, and I have been broken, but I am still in one piece, and I am here living a happy life. You can too. I hope my story helps.

Sources

http://www.nimh.nih.gov/health/statistics/prevalence/major-depression-among-adolescents.shtml

https://www.ineedalighthouse.org/depression-suicide/teen-depression/ http://www.safehorizon.org/page/homeless-youth-statistics--facts-69.html

http://kidshealth.org/en/teens/depression-tips.html?WT.ac=t-ra http://kidshealth.org/en/teens/rejection.html

http://www.usnews.com/education/blogs/high-school-notes/2015/01/19/help-high-schoolers-move-past-rejection-with-optimism

http://mom.me/kids/5369-attachment-theory-rejection-teenagers/ http://changingminds.org/explanations/behaviors/coping/coping.htm https://www.semel.ucla.edu/dual-diagnosis-program/News_and_Resources/How_Do_You_Cope http://www.helpguide.org/articles/depression/teen-depression-signs-help.htm http://articles.philly.com/2016-02-14/news/70596213_1_teen-prostitute-group-home-witness

http://www.1800runaway.org/2012/11/im-18-and-homeless-what-are-my-housing-options/

Other Books by Patrice M Foster

1. A guide to teenage depression
2. Left across the Border series 1
3. Tainted by Hate Series 3
4. The Journey Home A memoir

www.ingramcontent.com/pod-product-compliance
Lightning Source LLC
Chambersburg PA
CBHW030000290326
41935CB00008B/639

* 9 7 8 0 9 9 8 1 8 7 4 1 9 *